BONES
and
JOINTS

Brian Ward

FRANKLIN WATTS

New York/London/Toronto/Sydney

© Franklin Watts 1991

Franklin Watts, Inc.
387 Park Avenue South
New York, NY 10016

Library of Congress Cataloging-in-Publication Data

Ward, Brian R.
    Bones and joints / Brian Ward.
        p.   cm. — (Health guides)
    Includes index.
    Summary: Examines injuries and diseases likely to afflict the
bones and joints, including breaks, strains, arthritis, and cancer.
    ISBN 0-531-14175-6
    1. Bones—Wounds and injuries—Juvenile literature.   2. Joints—
Wounds and injuries—Juvenile literature.   3. Sports—Accidents and
injuries—Juvenile literature.   4. Bones—Diseases—Juvenile
literature.   5. Joints—Diseases—Juvenile literature.   [1. Bones—
Wounds and injuries.   2. Joints—Wounds and injuries.   3. Bones—
Diseases.   4. Joints—Diseases.]   I. Title.   II. Series: Ward,
Brian R. Health guides.
RD101.W187   1991
617.4'71044—dc20   90-46111
                                                            CIP AC

Series editor: Sarah Ridley
Editor: Ros Mair
Design: K and Co
Consultant: Dr. Philip Sawney

Illustrations: Aziz Khan pg 6, 10, 14, 16, 18, 21, 22, 26

Photographs: Heather Angel 30b; thanks to Sue Wyson/Animal Health Trust 30t;
Chris Fairclough 4b, 18b; Chris Fairclough Colour Library 10bl, 16t, 17t, 19tl, 26t;
Robert Harding Picture Library 5tl, 5br, 22bl, 27br; Hutchison Library 19tr, 28bl, 29b;
thanks to Keep Able Ltd 25t; NHPA/Agence Nature 15b; Rex Features 9tl, 13t;
courtesy of the Trustees of the Science Museum, London 15t; Science Photo Library
4t, 5bl, 7tl, 7tr, 7b, 8t, 9tr, 9b, 10br, 13b 20bl, 22br, 23b, 24b, 25b, 28br; Eileen
Langsley/Supersport front cover, 5tr, 12br, 17c, 17br, 28t, 29tl, 29tr; John Watney
Photo Library 8b, 20br, 21t, 21b, 24t, 27t; ZEFA 11, 14br, 19b, 27bl.

Printed in Belgium

CONTENTS

FEELING GOOD

Your skeleton supports and protects your body. Although it is made from hard bone, there is a lot you can do to improve the strength of your skeleton, and to keep the joints that allow you to move supple and strong.

An adequate diet will supply the minerals which are essential to healthy bone growth, and exercise keeps the bones strong and the joints healthy. There are three different kinds of physical fitness which improve the health of your skeleton and joints.

Strength means that the muscles moving the bones have become very efficient. Exercise that develops your strength also makes the bones and joints much stronger.

Stamina is the ability to continue exercising for a long time without getting tired. This too will strengthen your bones.

Suppleness is the ability to move all the joints freely, without causing any pain or damage.

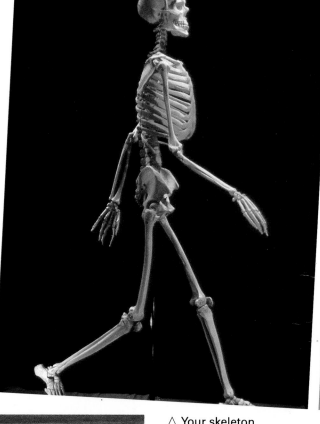

△ Your skeleton supports you, protects your vital organs, and at the same time allows great freedom of movement. Although your skeleton is made of hard bone, you can improve its strength and mobility by getting plenty of the right kinds of exercise.

◁ Jogging (in moderation) strengthens the legs and makes the joints more supple. It is important to wear a good pair of running shoes as otherwise you can cause stress to your muscles and skeleton.

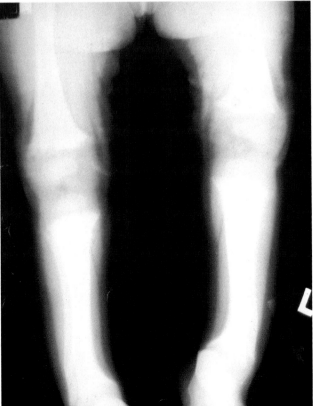

(top left) Weightlifting makes you strong, but can damage joints.

◁ Rickets, caused by poor diet or lack of sunlight, can deform leg bones.

△ Gymnasts develop very free-moving joints which allow them flexibility.

▽ Swimming exercises almost all the muscles and joints in the body.

THE SKELETON

The skeleton is a very effective device to protect the vital body organs, while at the same time allowing us to move very freely. It is composed of bone, which is hard and extremely strong. There are 206 bones in the adult body, but we are born with 350 bones, and some of these fuse together.

The skull is a rounded structure made up from several separate bones which fuse permanently. It protects the brain, eyes and hearing organs from damage, and because of its rounded shape, is very strong.

The spine, supporting the skull, is also strong. It has the essential function of protecting the spinal cord, a thick mass of nerves which is encased within a long line of 33 bony vertebrae. These small bones are joined in such a way that the spine can flex without damaging the spinal cord inside.

The heart and lungs are also surrounded by a bony structure. The ribs form a wall around them, and also play an important part in breathing.

The whole weight of the body is carried by the legs, which are connected to the spine by the pelvis. The arms do not have to be as strong as the legs, so their connections to the spine are more flexible, allowing freer movement. The fingers and toes contain many small bones which allow them to move when we grasp objects or walk and run.

▽ The bones of the skeleton are shaped according to their uses. The thighbones carry most of the weight of the body, and are extremely rigid, while the ribs are springy and so allow the chest to expand when you breathe.

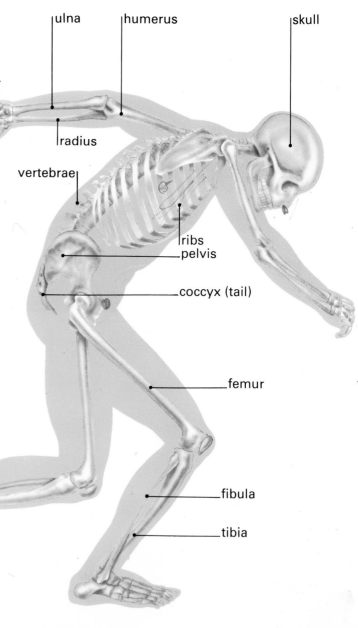

ulna humerus skull

radius

vertebrae

ribs
pelvis

coccyx (tail)

femur

fibula

tibia

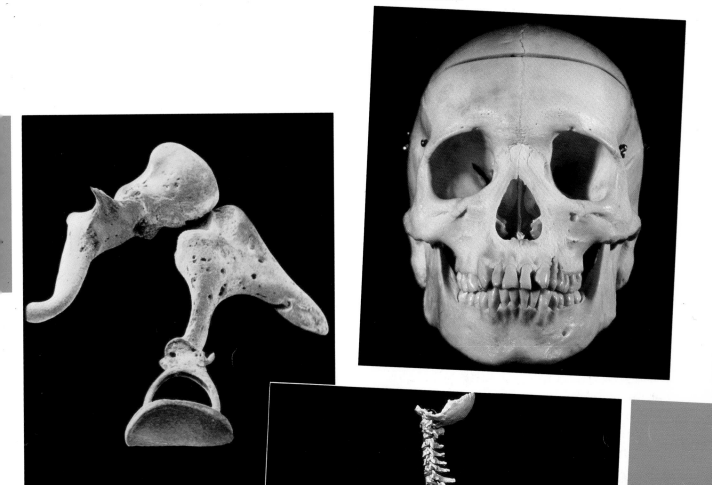

△ The ear bones (shown here greatly enlarged) are the smallest bones in the body. They carry sound to the inner ear. Vibrations move the malleus (hammer) at top left, which strikes the incus (anvil), finally passing on the sound to the stapes (stirrup) at the bottom of the picture. This bone transfers the vibration into the receptor part of the ear.

(top right) The skull is formed from several bones permanently joined together (these fixed joints are the zigzag lines you can see on this skull). The rounded part of the skull covers and protects the brain, while sense organs of sight and smell are at the front, where they are most useful.

▷ This picture shows the whole length of the spine, and how it connects to the pelvis. The strongest vertebrae are at the lower part of the spine, to carry the most weight.

LIVING BONE

Although bone seems hard and stonelike, it is a flexible, living substance. Bone cells deposit the hard bone tissue around themselves, in layers like an onion. The bone is composed of minerals (mainly calcium and phosphorus) and is further strengthened by fibers of a tough flexible substance called collagen. Bone is one of the toughest natural substances, and a cubic inch of bone could support the weight of five large cars. The outer layer of a bone is very hard, to provide strength, but the inner part is spongelike, which keeps the weight down. Long bones in the limbs contain marrow, where red and white blood cells are produced.

The skeleton begins to form from rubbery cartilage, and as we grow, this is slowly replaced by hard bone. A baby's arms and

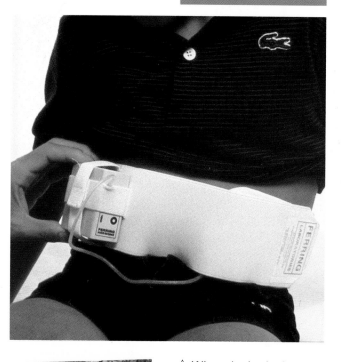

△ When the body does not produce enough growth hormone in childhood, growth may be slowed. Giving the hormone to these children can restore normal growth rates. One method is to wear a special device which steadily pumps tiny amounts of hormone into the body through a hypodermic needle.

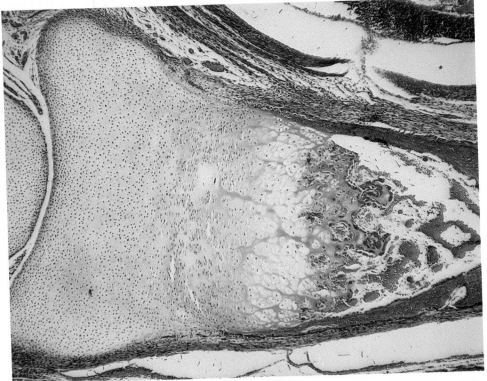

◁ In this cross-section of a developing bone, the hard part of the bone is the dark red area. The green part is cartilage at the end of the bone, where growth is taking place. The new cartilage is gradually changed into hard bone as growth continues.

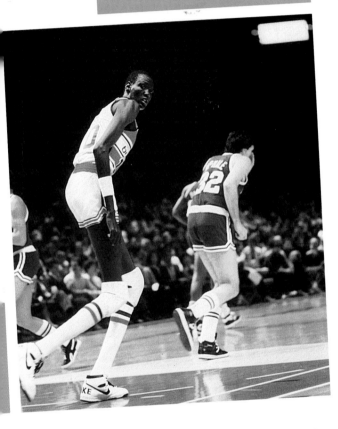

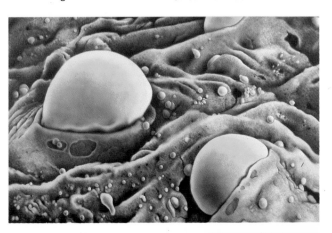

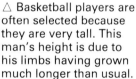

△ Basketball players are often selected because they are very tall. This man's height is due to his limbs having grown much longer than usual.

▽ Immature blood cells are produced from the bone marrow inside hollow bones. They develop to become red or white blood cells.

△ This eleven-year-old boy is very short for his age because his pituitary gland is not producing enough growth hormone. The growth hormone treatment he receives will make all his bones grow at the normal speed, and his height will soon catch up with other children.

legs are very short, but the bones lengthen as the cells in the bone ends multiply. Eventually all the cartilage is replaced by bone, except for small amounts at the ends of some bones. Some people suffer from diseases which affect the hormones stimulating bone growth. Very short children can grow to normal size if they are treated with growth hormone. Other children may become giants if too much growth hormone is produced in their bodies.

JOINTS

Where bone meets bone the body has joints. Some joints are permanently fixed, such as those in the separate bony plates of the skull. But most joints allow movement, and their structure varies depending on the sort of movement they are made for. For example, the vertebrae in the spine allow only limited movement, when the disks of rubbery cartilage separating them are compressed. This lack of movement ensures the safety of the delicate spinal cord.

Joints are designed so that they can maintain themselves and repair themselves if they are damaged, unless they become diseased. The main joints of the body are synovial joints. This means that between the cartilage-covered ends of the bones, there is a capsule, or bag, containing oily, slippery synovial fluid to reduce wear and tear.

The jointed bones are held together by ligaments. These are tough flexible strands which keep the ends of the bone firmly

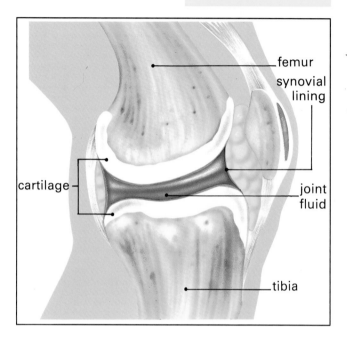

femur

synovial lining

cartilage

joint fluid

tibia

▽ Jugglers must have very fit muscles and joints to allow them to move quickly. In yoga, loose and flexible joints are more important.

△ Synovial joints contain oily fluid in a bag between the cartilage at the ends of bones. This reduces friction and wear.

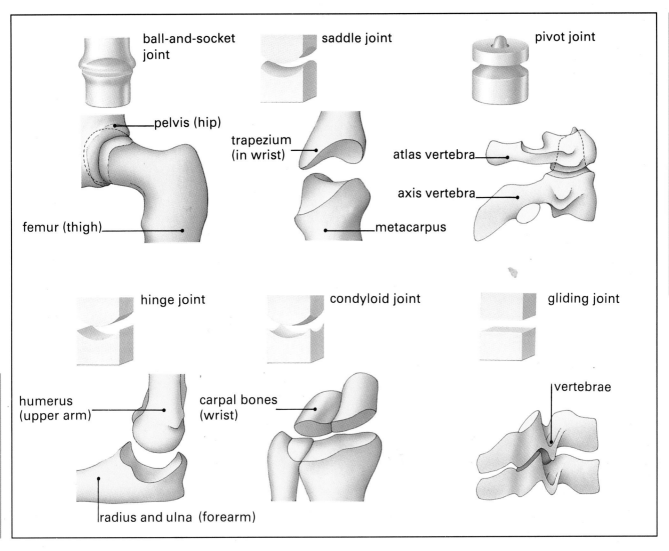

ball-and-socket joint

pelvis (hip)

femur (thigh)

saddle joint

trapezium (in wrist)

metacarpus

pivot joint

atlas vertebra

axis vertebra

hinge joint

humerus (upper arm)

radius and ulna (forearm)

condyloid joint

carpal bones (wrist)

gliding joint

vertebrae

△ Joints connect two or more bones together. There are several types of joint in the body. Each allows the bones a certain range of movement, but also prevents them from moving in the wrong direction.

▷ Playing the violin or other stringed instruments requires flexible fingers which can reach a long way into unaccustomed positions. This requires long training and practice, as well as a good deal of strength.

together, while allowing the joint to move in the proper directions. Strong, healthy muscles also keep the bones together.

The structure of a joint allows it to work only in a particular way. Hinge joints like those in the elbow give a simple to-and-fro movement, but the whole limb can achieve many different actions using other joints.

MUSCLES

All body movement is caused by the action of muscles. A muscle consists of a bundle of small fibers, which is joined by a tough ropy tendon to another bone or tissue, such as the skin on the face. The muscle shortens or contracts when it receives an electrical signal from a nerve. It pulls on the bone or other organ, and causes it to move. In fact, a muscle can only pull, so to reverse the movement, another muscle must pull back in the opposite direction. These pairs are called opposed muscles. They keep the joint together, and they are usually lightly contracted. This produces muscle tone, which means that they don't become floppy when they are not being used.

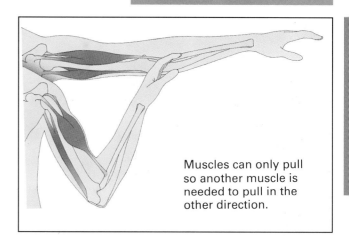

Muscles can only pull so another muscle is needed to pull in the other direction.

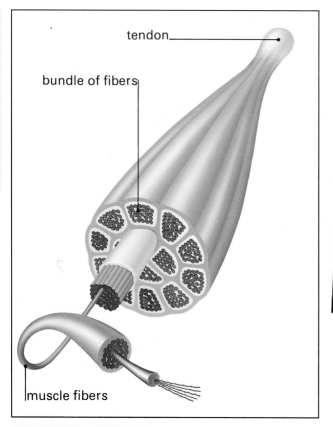

tendon

bundle of fibers

muscle fibers

◁ Muscles are made of bundles of muscle fibers. These shorten and make the muscle contract when they receive nerve messages.

△ Muscular strength, suppleness and stamina are all important to gymnasts, who must support their whole weight on their arms.

The muscle fibers are long cells containing two types of still smaller fibers. When an electrical impulse from the nervous system tells the muscle to contract, these fibers slide past each other, shortening the muscle fiber and the whole muscle. We cannot vary the amount of contraction of an individual muscle fiber, but our nervous system can instruct more or fewer fibers to contract so we can make small, delicate movements, or more powerful movements, as they are needed. The body contains more than 600 of these voluntary muscles. Other types of muscles are called involuntary, as they work automatically. These muscles make the heart beat, and move food through the digestive system.

(top right) Facial expressions are made by muscles attached to skin. ▽ This picture shows the immense muscular effort needed in pole vaulting.

▷ Muscles are attached all around the eye. This allows the eye to be swiveled in any direction, rotating in the eye socket.

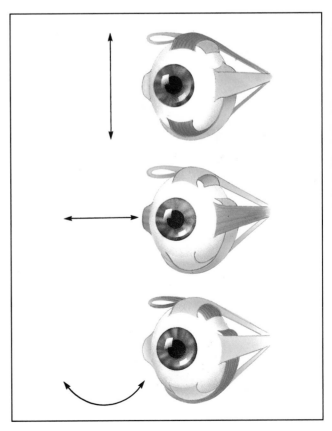

THE WORKING SKELETON

A simple movement like walking is not really simple for the body. Many joints and muscles must work together in perfect harmony in order for you to take each step. As you step forward, the muscles in your thigh lift your leg. At the same time, your abdominal muscles tighten, and you push forward using the muscles in your other leg. All this is complicated enough, but if these were the only muscles in use, you would lose your balance and fall over. Your body is constantly making small adjustments, involving muscles from your neck right down to your feet. You can check this for yourself by using your fingertips to feel the muscles shifting beneath your skin as you walk or run.

The loads that the skeleton carries when running or jumping can be very heavy. As you run, the heel strikes the ground first, and the

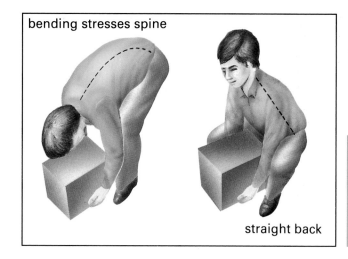

bending stresses spine

straight back

▽ When you run, your heel hits the ground hard. The shock travels up your legs and spine, and is cushioned by bent limbs and cartilage between the bones.

△ Bending over to lift heavy loads could damage your back. It is better to keep your back straight and use the strength in your legs to provide the lift.

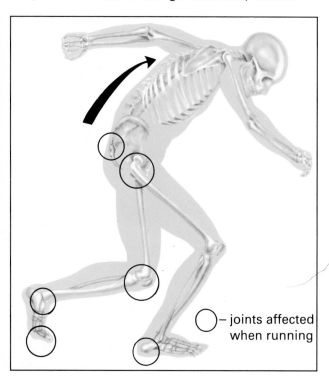

— joints affected when running

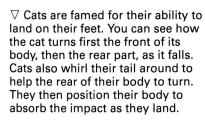

▽ Cats are famed for their ability to land on their feet. You can see how the cat turns first the front of its body, then the rear part, as it falls. Cats also whirl their tail around to help the rear of their body to turn. They then position their body to absorb the impact as they land.

△ These historic photographs were among the first to show in detail how the body moves during normal activities. This series of pictures shows how we lean forward as we step up a stair.

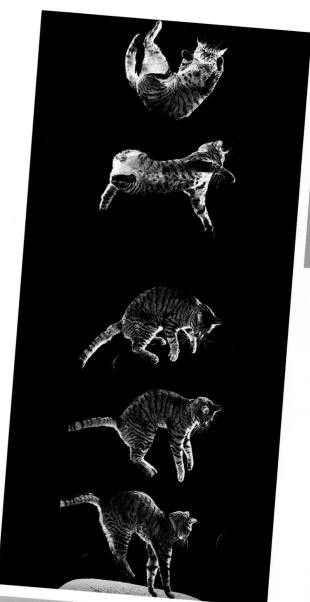

impact travels up your legs and your spine. The thighbone may have to withstand a force of a ton or more, for a few movements. Most of the impact is absorbed by the rubbery cartilage cushioning each joint, and also by the bending of your legs. If you ever fall a short distance and land on your straightened legs, as can happen if you slip off a stair, you will experience the shock of this impact – it travels right up your spine, and can cause your jaw to shut with a painful click.

STRAINS AND SPRAINS

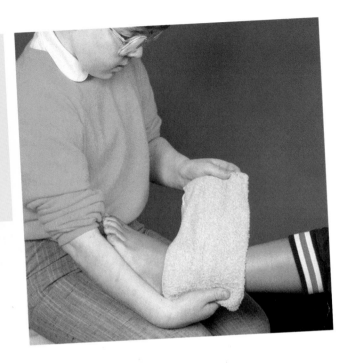

Joints are designed for a particular type of movement, and the amount they move is limited by their structure. If a joint is flexed too far, it becomes painful. This is a natural warning that the ligaments holding the joint together are being stretched, and the pain usually stops you from damaging the joint by bending it any further.

Sometimes people slip and fall awkwardly, and the joint is stretched beyond its limits. This usually happens to an ankle, but it could happen to any moveable joint. The wrench flexes the joint too far, and the ligaments tear, causing severe pain. At the same time, some of the tissue around the joint is damaged, as the bones are levered a short distance apart, and blood escapes into the damaged joint. The immediate reaction of the body is to mobilize the repair mechanisms. Chemicals are produced from the damaged tissue which

△ Sprains are best treated with a cold compress, provided this can be applied before the joint is seriously swollen. The cold compress is simply a towel or piece of cloth, soaked in cold water (with ice, if possible), which is wrapped around the damaged area as quickly as possible after the injury. The low temperature makes the blood vessels around the area narrow, and restrict the blood flow. This reduces the leakage of blood and other fluid into the wound, so swelling is reduced.

▷ Most of the pain caused by a sprain results from swelling and inflammation in the joint, causing pressure. Any attempt to walk on a sprained ankle will make the damage worse, so it must be rested until it is no longer painful. Overuse before healing is complete can mean that ligaments are permanently damaged, and the joint made unstable.

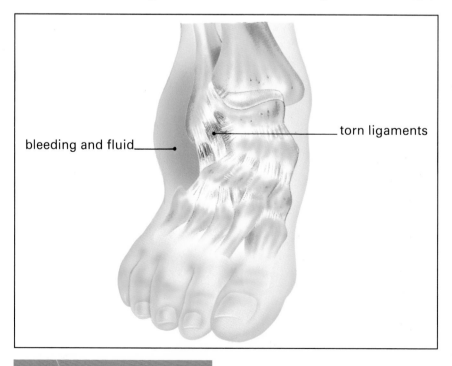

bleeding and fluid — torn ligaments

First Aid

Remove shoe if the ankle is damaged.

Put the affected part into cold water, or wrap a cold wet cloth loosely around it.

Immobilize the joint to prevent further damage and elevate the ankle above the hips to reduce the swelling.

Take acetaminophen at the recommended dose to control the pain.

You **must** go to a doctor or to the hospital if the joint is very painful and swollen, to make sure the bone is not fractured or the joint dislocated.

◁ This athlete is wearing a support for a strained muscle. This injury is caused by overuse of the muscle, and some fibers have been torn.

▽ Muscle strains can be caused by putting too much strain on muscles before they are properly prepared. This is why athletes "limber up" with stretching exercises.

△ Contact sports like soccer and rugby always carry some risk of injury. Sprains, strains, and broken bones are the most common types of injury, and damage to the cartilage of a joint has finished the careers of many sportsmen. Clubs have physiotherapists to help their players regain full fitness.

cause inflammation. The damaged area becomes swollen as fluid leaks from the tissues, carrying with it various types of white blood cells, which begin to "mop up" damaged cells. The whole joint may feel hot and very painful while all this is going on. Fortunately, a sprain or strain heals quickly, given rest.

Strains are tears in a muscle, usually caused by using a lot of force while in an awkward position. They are very painful but do not usually require treatment, as they heal by themselves in a few days.

DISLOCATIONS

In dislocations the bones are forced so far that they lever the joint apart, tearing the ligaments, damaging the joint capsule, and causing damage to the cartilage in the joint and the muscles and tendons around it. This condition is so painful that most people with a dislocation will not attempt to move themselves before medical help arrives.

In some bad dislocations, the structure of the joint may be irreparably damaged, but in general they can be repaired surgically. The parts of the joint are put back in their proper positions, and held there while healing takes place. This usually means surgery, carried out under an anesthetic, and a plaster cast or some other form of splint to hold the joint immobile for at least three weeks. In most cases recovery is complete, but sometimes the joint is weakened. Dislocations are common in football players and those playing

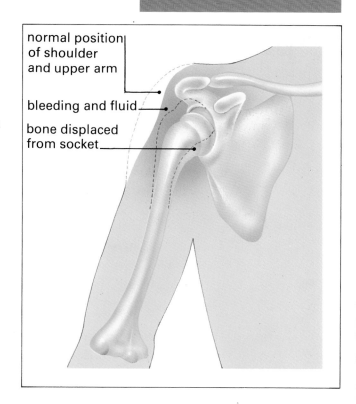

normal position of shoulder and upper arm

bleeding and fluid

bone displaced from socket

△ Dislocations are very serious injuries in which a bone is pulled or levered right out of the socket, damaging and sometimes destroying the surrounding tissues. There is a lot of bleeding into the joint, which becomes very swollen and is extremely painful.

◁ Football is another contact sport in which injuries such as dislocations can occur. Players are selected partly because of their size and weight, and this also increases the chance of serious injury. Unlike soccer or rugby, protective armor is worn to reduce the risk.

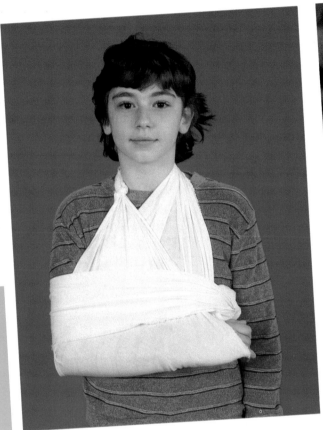

△ This boy has developed amazingly supple joints which allow him to contort himself into positions that are normally impossible.

△ Dislocated joints must be rested as they heal, and a sling will help.

▷ Babies have very loose joints, and can bend more freely than adults.

other "contact" sports.

Many people are said to be "double-jointed," and seem to be able to dislocate their joints at will, without causing any damage. You can see this effect with babies, who can bend into positions that would be impossible for an older child. This is because the ligaments in a baby are much softer and more elastic than those of an older child, so the bones of a joint can flex more than usual. Some athletes can maintain exceptional joint flexibility by constant exercise.

HEALING BONES

Bones are very strong, but they can break if certain types of load are applied to them. Most breaks or fractures are caused by falls. In children and adults, a very common fracture happens to the small bones in the wrist, or the radius or ulna bones in the forearm. These fractures are the result of an instinctive attempt to break the fall, using the hands. A much more serious fracture in later years is to break off the head of the thigh-bone, where it joins onto the hip. This often happens with a fall, because in older people, bones have become brittle.

There are several different types of fracture, but the most common is the simple fracture when a bone is cleanly snapped. In a compound fracture, the bone is broken and the sharp edges may protrude through the skin. This is serious, since bacteria may enter, and could cause a bone infection.

Because bone is a living tissue, it will repair itself if the broken parts are kept together without shifting. Much of the healing takes place in the periosteum, the thin layer of blood vessels and nerves covering the bone. The whole area becomes inflamed as the healing process cleans away dead and damaged tissue and new cells move into the fracture to make the repair. Eventually, this part of the bone will be stronger than all the rest, as a thickened layer of bone called callus is built up over the damaged area.

(far right) A compound fracture can be serious. This X-ray shows that the tibia and fibula have both broken, and have splintered. On the right of the picture is tissue damage where the ends of the bone may have poked out through the skin. In this type of injury, a metal plate may be screwed to the bones to hold them into position while they heal.

▷ This X-ray picture shows a simple fracture in the tibia, the bone at the front of the shin, while the thinner fibula bone is undamaged. The bone has snapped cleanly across, and although it will be painful and swollen, there will not be great damage to the surrounding tissue. This kind of fracture heals quickly, and the bone will soon be as strong as ever.

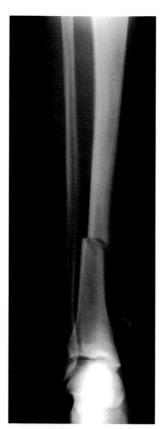
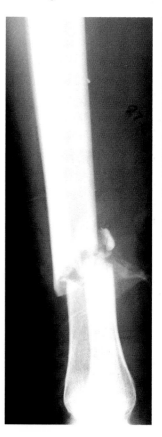

First Aid

Never try to move anyone who seems to have a break or fracture. If you try to straighten an arm or leg you could cause further damage. Cover up the casualty to keep him or her warm, and send for help at once.

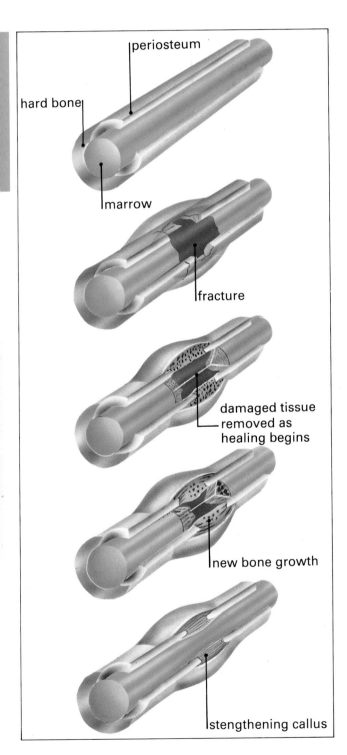

periosteum

hard bone

marrow

fracture

damaged tissue removed as healing begins

new bone growth

stengthening callus

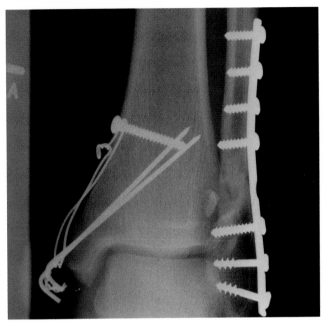

◁ The repair process begins as blood cells clean up the damage around the fracture, and new bone forms a strengthening callus.

△ Metal plates, screws and wires are used to repair this bad fracture. ▽ Fractured limbs are immobilized with plaster while the bone heals.

BACK INJURIES

Nearly everyone suffers from back pain at some time during their lives. The spinal column is a very complicated structure, immensely strong yet flexible. Its vertebrae interlock so as to protect the spinal cord, but they allow limited movement. They are braced by many muscles, ligaments and tendons. If you lift something heavy, all of its weight is added to the weight of your body, pressing down on the spine. If you keep your spine straight, this should not cause a problem, but if you bend over to lift, the spine comes under extra strain. A torn muscle or stretched ligament is the most likely cause of pain.

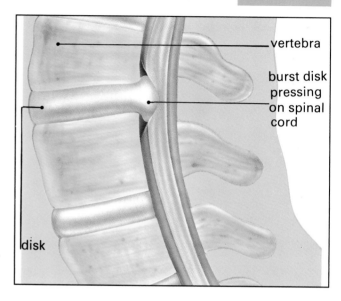

vertebra

burst disk pressing on spinal cord

disk

◁ Good posture means keeping the head up, shoulders back, the back straight, and the belly tucked in. This is the healthiest position for the spine.
▽ A surgical collar takes the strain off the neck after a spinal injury.

△ The rubbery disks of cartilage between the vertebrae are strong, but they can be damaged. The disk splits or bursts, and presses against the nerves emerging between the vertebrae, or may press on the spinal cord.

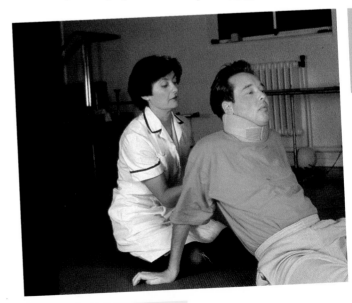

A "slipped disk" is a more serious problem. Disks of rubbery cartilage separate each vertebra, allowing a small amount of movement and cushioning impacts. If very strong loads are applied to the spine while it is in an awkward position, the disk may burst, and its jellylike contents are squeezed out. The result may be that a nerve branching out from the spinal cord at that point is pinched, and causes pain. Or the damaged disk may squeeze against the spinal cord itself, and affect its functioning.

A fracture of the spine can completely cut the spinal cord, producing paralysis. This sort of injury is associated with certain sports.

First Aid
NEVER attempt to move anyone who seems to have a back or neck injury, as this could cause serious and permanent damage. It is important to keep the casualty as still as possible, by very lightly packing clothes or blankets around them while you send for medical help.

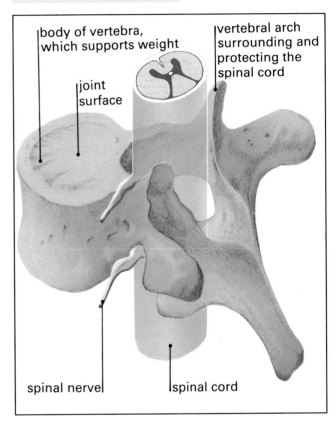

body of vertebra, which supports weight

vertebral arch surrounding and protecting the spinal cord

joint surface

spinal nerve

spinal cord

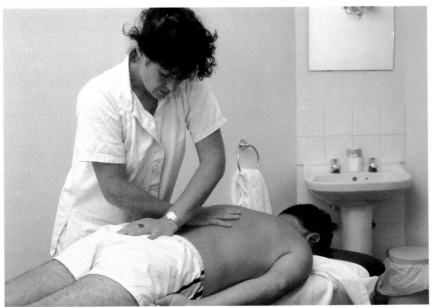

△ The vertebrae which make up the spine are very complicated in shape, because they have special functions. They link together, and are interlocked to give them extra strength. Weight is supported on the rounded bodies of the vertebrae, which are separated by the rubbery vertebral disk. Muscles and ligaments are attached to "wings" which stick out from the vertebrae, and they contain a hole for the spinal cord.

◁ There are many conditions which can cause back pain, and sometimes this lingers on and causes great inconvenience and restricted movement. Massage helps in some types of back pain, although it must be done properly to avoid causing further damage. Osteopaths treat various aches and pains by massaging in a special way.

JOINT DISEASE

There are many diseases of joints, and these usually affect older people. The most common joint disease is a kind of arthritis known as osteoarthritis. It is thought to be caused by wear and tear on the joint. The rubbery cartilage on the tips of the bones gradually becomes thinner and wears away. As this happens, the joint becomes stiff and painful until eventually, the ends of the bone itself become worn and the joint may not be capable of use at all. Osteoarthritis is common in people who do heavy manual work, or those who are very overweight, putting an extra load on the joints in their legs.

The other common form of joint disease is rheumatoid arthritis. In this condition, the joints become inflamed and very swollen. The inflammation damages the capsule holding lubricating synovial fluid, and the

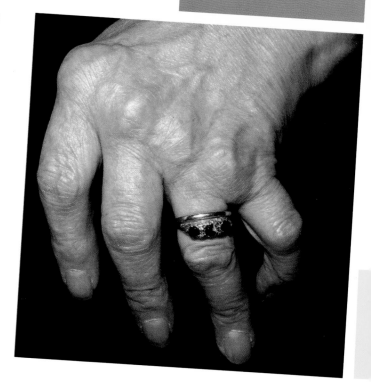

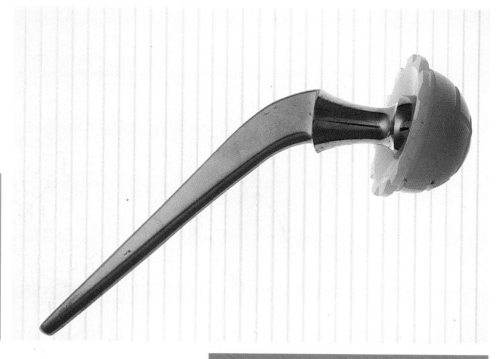

△ Rheumatoid arthritis can attack any joint but is particularly noticeable in the hands. Arthritic joints are destroyed and the hands can become distorted with the fingers twisted to one side. Modern treatments can help to minimize these deformities.

◁ This is a replacement hipbone, which will be implanted into the hip of someone with severe arthritis. The metal spike is bonded into the hollow end of the femur, and the plastic cup end is attached to the pelvis. This restores almost normal movement, and lasts for years.

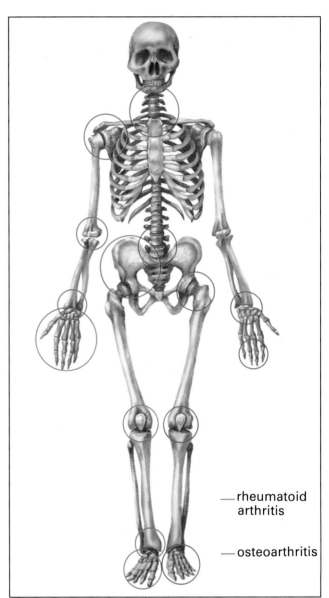

— rheumatoid arthritis

— osteoarthritis

△ These faucets have been specially designed to help people with arthritis. *(bottom right)* This special X-ray of arthritic hands shows healthy bone in yellow, while areas weakened by rheumatoid arthritis show up as a bluish-green color.

▷ Osteoarthritis and rheumatoid arthritis both affect the joints, but different types of joint may be involved. Osteoarthritis usually affects the joints that work hardest, but rheumatoid arthritis damages any joint, and may affect other organs.

joint eventually locks up and cannot be used. The causes are not well understood, but it is thought that the body's defense systems have mistakenly begun to attack healthy tissue. This also affects other parts of the body, and may make sufferers feel weak and ill.

Arthritis is treated with drugs, but sometimes the damage is so severe that an artificial replacement joint must be fitted.

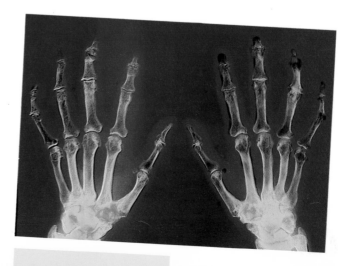

BONE AGING

During our lives, all the cells in the body die and are replaced several times over (apart from the nerve cells). Bone tissue is constantly being absorbed and replaced by fresh bone. The processes must be kept in exact balance, and are controlled by hormones. But as we get older, the bone replacement slows down, and total bone loss starts to increase. The loss of calcium means that the bone becomes more spongelike, and the hard surface layer becomes thinner. In addition, the reinforcing strands of collagen in the bone gradually disappear, leaving the bone further weakened.

This thinning of the bone is called osteoporosis, and it significantly weakens the bone. It is more common in women who are in

△ Some elderly people get shorter as they grow older. This is due to thinning of the cartilage disks between the vertebrae, and also the gradual collapse of the vertebrae themselves. This is caused by a condition called osteoporosis, when calcium is lost from bones, so they become brittle.

▷ The inside of healthy bone is naturally like a honeycomb, with a hard layer on the surface of the bone. The honeycomb structure is very strong and rigid, but is also light. As bone is lost in older people, the cavities inside the bone become larger, and eventually the bone is left brittle and weak, and liable to fracture.

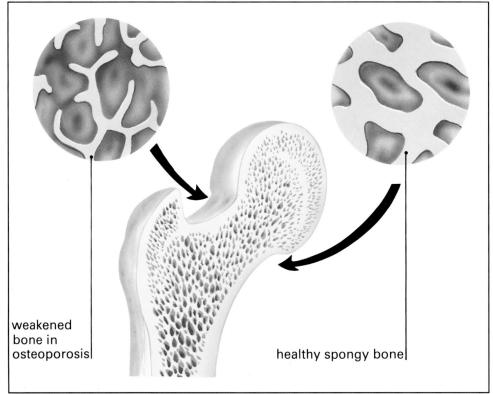

weakened bone in osteoporosis

healthy spongy bone

◁ Calcium is an important part of our bones, and is needed to replace that lost by natural processes. Calcium loss increases in elderly people, so it is important that they eat and drink foods that will help replace it. Dairy products, legumes, bread, fresh green vegetables and fish are all high in calcium, and are important for both young and old people.

▽ Osteoporosis can cause dangerous bone loss in the elderly, making their bones very brittle. One reason for this is the reduction in the amount of a hormone called calcitonin. This substance can be replaced by calcitonin extracted from salmon, eels, or other animals, and when given to people, it may help to restore strength to their bones.

△ The body reacts to exercise by making the bones stronger. Exercise is particularly important for older people to prevent the strength of their bones from deteriorating.

their menopause, the time in a woman's life when her ovaries stop releasing egg cells, and the production of hormones decreases. The condition is less common in elderly men.

We obtain calcium from our diet and it is particularly important for old people to get enough calcium to replace that being lost through osteoporosis. Some drugs that replace hormones formerly produced by the body can stop the process of osteoporosis.

HEALTHY BODIES

A good diet while you are young helps to make sure that your body takes in sufficient calcium and other minerals to produce strong, healthy bones. Exercise also has important effects on the bones and joints. In older people, exercise can stop the process of bone loss, or osteoporosis, so the bones may become strong again. In young people, the right kind of exercise helps the bones to grow and remain healthy, and keeps the joints supple. Constant use of a joint stretches its ligaments slightly, allowing it to bend freely. You can see this happening most easily with the spine, when you attempt to touch your toes. At first this may be difficult but with practice you will be able to rest your palms flat on the floor.

Dance exercise, aerobics, yoga and swimming all flex the joints and will improve

◁ Tennis elbow is a painful condition caused by inflammation where a tendon attaches to bone near the elbow.
(bottom left) Exercise can be fun too, and can be shared with friends.

▽ Disability does not stop people from enjoying exercise. These disabled athletes have developed powerful shoulders and arms to compensate for their inability to use their legs.

△ Keep fit is very popular, and has now grown to be a form of dance.
◁ With training, some elderly people can take part in strenuous sports such as running.

▽ T'ai chi, very popular in the Far East, is a form of fitness training, which improves joint suppleness. It is carried out very slowly, so it can be enjoyed even by very old people.

your suppleness. But with these or any other forms of exercise, you must stop immediately if you suffer any pain. This is a warning that you are working your joints and muscles too hard, and if you continue you could tear a ligament. After a while, you will notice that you can bend your joints further than before.

On the other hand, too much exercise of the wrong kind can cause lasting damage. Some young athletes and tennis players have "worn out" their joints and developed osteoarthritis at a very young age.

SPECIALIZED BONES

Although all warm-blooded animals are built to the same general plan, their skeletons have adapted to their needs. Our own arms, for example, give us the ability to handle objects with great skill, and to make and use tools in an intelligent way. This distinguishes us from all other living creatures. Whales and dolphins have "arms" with the same basic structure as our own but with short "arm" bones and very long "fingers," making a flipper which helps them in swimming. In horses, the "finger" bones are fused together to make a strong hoof which they need for running.

If you look at the skeleton of any mammal or bird, you will see similarities in the structure, even when the whole animal looks very different from us. A giraffe only has seven neck bones, as we have, but they are obviously very much bigger than ours. Most animals have tails, and so do we. The human "tail" is a short section of tiny vertebrae fused together, at the bottom of the spine. It is called the coccyx, and in the course of evolution has lost its function and shrunk in size.

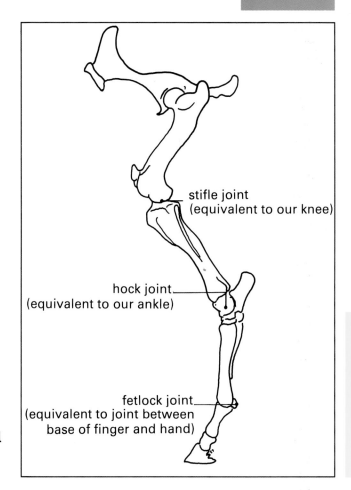

stifle joint (equivalent to our knee)

hock joint (equivalent to our ankle)

fetlock joint (equivalent to joint between base of finger and hand)

△ The horse runs on its "toes and fingertips." The bones of its hands and feet are fused together to make a strong hoof which can withstand the force of the horse galloping. It is covered with strong material adapted from fingernails.

◁ From its outside appearance, no one would think that the giraffe has the same number of bones in its neck as humans. In fact, nearly all vertebrate animals are built on roughly the same plan, with a skull, spine, and limbs. There are all kinds of modifications which suit the animal's way of life.

GLOSSARY

Arthritis: A painful condition by which the joints become inflamed and stiff, and may lock solidly after several years.

Calcium: A mineral substance which is the most important part of bone, making it hard and rigid. Calcium is also important to the proper functioning of muscles and nerves.

Cartilage: A rubbery substance which is used to support and protect the body from shocks and impacts. The ends of most bones are covered with cartilage to make a smooth, flexible joint.

Coccyx: The last few vertebrae in the spine are fused together to make a "tail," called the coccyx.

Collagen: This is a very strong but flexible substance which is present in joints as bands which hold the joint together, but allow it to move freely.

Disk: Between the vertebrae are springy disks which allow the spine to bend, and absorb the stresses caused by running and walking.

Fracture: A break in a bone is called a fracture. The bone can break across, split or sometimes break into several small pieces.

Hormone: The body controls many of its functions by means of chemical messengers or hormones. These substances are produced in special endocrine glands, and carried around the body in the blood.

Joint: Where two or more bones meet. Most joints allow the bones to move, but some, like those in the skull, are rigidly fixed.

Ligament: Tough bands of collagen which hold a joint together.

Marrow: Soft spongy material inside the largest bones of the body. New blood cells are produced in the bone marrow.

Mineral: Substance obtained from food, which is used in many organs and body tissues.

Muscle: Tissue composed of thin muscle fibers, which shorten or contract when they receive a message from the nervous system. Some types of muscle work automatically to maintain the body. Others only work when movement is needed.

Nerve/nervous system: Nerves are bundles of tiny thread-like cells which convey messages to and from the brain, in the form of a very small electrical impulse. The brain and spinal cord, together with nerves, make up the nervous system.

Osteoporosis: In this condition, the mineral calcium in the bone is lost, so the bones become brittle and break easily.

Skeleton: The framework of 206 bones which supports the body and protects vital organs.

Spine: The spine supports the upper part of the body. It consists of a series of vertebrae which are jointed so that the spine can bend, while still protecting the spinal cord which runs inside it.

Synovial fluid: The slippery fluid which lubricates joints.

Tendon: Tough, ropy strand which connects muscles to bone.

Vertebrae: Small ring-like bones which are joined together to make the spine. Their shape is complicated as they must make the spine strong, yet allow it to move and protect the spinal cord.

INDEX

PRINTED IN BELGIUM BY
proost
INTERNATIONAL BOOK PRODUCTION